The Le

Su

methuen | drama

LONDON · NEW YORK · OXFORD · NEW DELHI · SYDNEY

METHUEN DRAMA
Bloomsbury Publishing Plc
50 Bedford Square, London, WC1B 3DP, UK
1385 Broadway, New York, NY 10018, USA
29 Earlsfort Terrace, Dublin 2, Ireland

BLOOMSBURY, METHUEN DRAMA and the Methuen
Drama logo are trademarks of Bloomsbury Publishing Plc

First published in Great Britain 2024

A catalogue record for this book is available from the British Library.

Library of Congress Control Number: 2024950937

ISBN: PB: 978-1-3505-5166-4
ePDF: 978-1-3505-5167-1
eBook: 978-1-3505-5168-8

Series: Modern Plays

Typeset by Mark Heslington Ltd, Scarborough, North Yorkshire
Printed and bound in Great Britain

To find out more about our authors and books visit
www.bloomsbury.com and sign up for our newsletters.

THE ROYAL COURT THEATRE PRESENTS
A HACKNEY SHOWROOM PRODUCTION
ORIGINATED WITH BRIXTON HOUSE

The Legends of Them

By Sutara Gayle AKA Lorna Gee

The Legends of Them was first performed at Brixton House on Thursday 14 September and at the Royal Court Jerwood Theatre Downstairs, Sloane Square on Thursday 5 December 2024.

The Legends of Them
Written & Performed by Sutara Gayle AKA Lorna Gee

Director & Co-Creator **Jo McInnes**
Dramaturg & Co-Creator **Nina Lyndon**
Costume Designer **Melissa Simon-Hartman**
Lighting Designer **Joshie Harriette**
Composer & Musical Director **Christella Litras**
Sound Designer **Elena Peña**
Projection Designer **Tyler Forward**
Video Artist **Daniel Batters**
Live Sound Consultant **Tony Gayle**
Associate Director **Sam Curtis Lindsay**
Associate Artist **Martina Laird**
Stage Manager **Phyllys Egharevba**
Deputy Stage Manager **Reuben Bojang**
Sound & Music Assistant **Christian Gayle**
Session Musicians **Leroy Johnson & Scratch Professor**

From the Royal Court, on this production:

Executive Producer **Steven Atkinson**
Stage Supervisor **Steve Evans**
Lighting Operator **Izzy Hobby**
Lead Producer **Hannah Lyall**
Lighting Supervisor **Lucinda Plummer**
Production Manager **Marius Rønning**
Lighting Programmer **Lizzie Skellett**
Company Manager **Mica Taylor**
Video Supervisor **Deanna Towli**

A Hackney Showroom production originated with Brixton House with support from Arts
Council England, National Theatre Generate Programme & Maria Björnson Memorial Fund.

The Royal Court, Hackney Showroom and Stage Management wish to thank the following for their help
with this production: Stuart Heyes, Gino Ricardo Green, Back of Yard Studios & IAM Music Studios.

Sutara Gayle AKA Lorna Gee
(Writer & Performer)

For the Royal Court: **Blest Be the Tie, Sugar Mummies, At the Table, Almost Nothing.**

Other theatre includes: **The Baker's Wife (Menier Chocolate Factory); Paradise, Nation (National); The Crucible (RSC); A Tale of Two Cities (Regent's Park Open Air); Tina: The Tina Turner Musical, Guys and Dolls (West End/Tour).**

Film includes: **Viral, Anthony, Carmilla, A Caribbean Dream, SuperBob, The Dark Night, Run Fatboy Run.**

Television includes: **Supacell, Black Cake, Magpie Murders, Outlander, Strike, Ghosts, Crongton, Silent Witness, Eastenders, Small Axe.**

Awards include: **Jimmy Lindsay Queen of Reggae Award, Chaaawaaa Radio Female Legend Award, Stereograph Foundation Global Rhodium Screen and Stage Award, BEFFTA and HiCrEc award for Outstanding Contribution to Reggae Music, Lovers Rock Gala Award for Contribution to Lovers Rock Music at The Brixton Academy, New York Reggae Tamika Award Best Female DJ, BBC Radio London Reggae Awards for Best Female Artist. Offie Award for Best Performance Piece (The Legends of Them).**

Reuben Bojang
(Deputy Stage Manager)

Theatre includes: **Kim's Convenience (Riverside Studios); The Marilyn Conspiracy, Whodunnit [Unrehearsed] 3, ANIMAL (&Tour), Pickle (Park); Tomorrow is already dead (Soho); The Legends of Them (Brixton House).**

Phyllys Egharevba
(Stage Manager)

Design for theatre includes: **Refilwe (Bernie Grants, NYT, Talawa); Sucker Punch (Queen's Theatre Hornchurch); Trouble in Butetown (Donmar); No More Mr Nice Guy (Camden People's); Eating Jeff (No-Table Productions); The Wonderful (Theatre Peckham); Helium (The Space); Twenty Twenty, in a word (Young Vic).**

As production manager, theatre includes: **Retrograde, Rise (Kiln); Mandela, She Venture & He Wins (Young Vic); The Wonderful (Theatre Peckham).**

As stage manager, theatre includes: **Flip (Fuel); Odyssey (National); Cake, Hamlet (Theatre Peckham); Home (Young Vic).**

As deputy stage manager, theatre includes: **Red Pitch (SohoPlace); Tambo & Bones (Stratford East).**

Tyler Forward
(Projection Designer)

For the Royal Court: **G.**

As designer, theatre includes: **A Midsummer Night's Dream, Sunday in the Park with George (Mack); Dorian The Musical (Southwark Playhouse); Redcliffe (Turbine); Diana The Musical Concert (Eventim Apollo); Trompe L'Oiel (The Other Palace); Loserville (Blackheath Halls); Our House (Albany); No Man's Island, Redemption, Mission (The Big House); Play, The Games (P&O Arvia); Silence (Donmar/Tara); Musical Theatre Showcase (Trinity Laban); Roles We'll Never Play, Close Quarters (RADA); Opening Up: The Mental Health Musical (Union); Thoroughly Modern Millie (Electric); Nor Woman Neither (Tristan Bates); Macbeth (Vanbrugh); Stoning Mary (George Bernard Shaw).**

As designer, exhibitions include: **Wes Anderson Asteroid City, Future Shock.**

As associate designer, theatre includes: **Belle Livingstone's 58th Street Country Club, Burlesque The Musical (UK Premiere); Carlos Acosta's Nutcracker, Once The Musical Concert, Spongebob The Musical (Tour); Umm Kulthum & The Goldern Era (Bahrain National & Ithra); King Lear (West End); The House With Chicken Legs (Tour); The Trials (Marlowe).**

As associate designer, exhibitions include: **French Dispatch.**

Tony Gayle
(Live Sound Consultant)

For the Royal Court: **The Living Newspaper, Shoe Lady, Poet in da Corner (& UK Tour).**

Other theatre includes: **Becoming Nancy, Playboy of the West Indies (Birmingham Rep); SuperYou (Leicester Curve); Play On! (Talawa/UK Tour); Next To Normal (West End & Donmar); Gatsby (American Repertory Theater); Two Strangers (Carry A Cake Across New York), (West End & Kiln); Shifters (Bush); The Lonely Londoners (Jermyn Street); High Times & Dirty Monsters (Liverpool Playhouse); My Neighbour Totoro (Barbican); Pygmalion, Sylvia, The 47th (Old Vic); Beneatha's Place (Young Vic); School Girls; Or, The African Mean Girls (Lyric Hammersmith); Greatest Days (UK Tour Disney's AIDA); Newsies (Troubadour, Wembley Park Theatre); Kinky Boots (New Wosley); Legally Blonde (Regent's Park); Get Up, Stand Up! - The Bob Marley Musical (Lyric); A Place For We (& Park), Running With Lions (& Lyric Hammersmith) (Talawa); Spring Awakening, and breathe (Almeida); The Wiz (Hope Mill Theatre); Gin Craze! (Royal & Derngate); Lazarus (King's Cross Theatre).**

Awards include: **Olivier Award – Best Sound Design, WhatsOnStage Awards, Black British Theatre Awards - Light & Sound Recognition Award.**

Christian Gayle (Sound & Music Assistant)

Music production includes: **TopBoy Netflix, Sony adverts.**

Joshie Harriette
(Lighting Designer)

Theatre includes: **The New Real (RSC); Wet Mess (BAC); The Princess and the Pea (Unicorn & New Vic); The House of MCR (Factory International Manchester); Evita (Leicester Curve); Nutcracker (Tuff Nut Jazz Club), Primetime (& Hayward Gallery) (Southbank); The Instrumentals (& Little Angel), Dream of Delphi Tour, (Queen Elizabeth Hall); Cake The Musical (The Other Palace & Lyric); Sucker Punch (UK Tour); Bear Snores On (Regent's Park Open Air); The Legends of Them (Brixton House); Eve and Cain (Queen's Hornchurch).**

Dance includes: **Dawns Y Ceirw (Theatre Genedlaethol Cymru), Legacy (RBO Outcast, (Scottish Ballet), Warrior Queens (Sadler's Wells), Say Something (National Dance Company Wales).**

Awards include: **Black British Theatre Award for Lighting Recognition.**

Martina Laird
(Associate Artist)

For the Royal Court: **Who Cares, Breath Boom.**

Theatre includes: **The New Real, Coriolanus, The White Devil, Three Hours After Marriage, Troilus & Cressida (RSC); The Five Wives of Maurice Pinder, Moon on a Rainbow Shawl (National); Meetings (Orange Tree); The Animal Kingdom (Hampstead); 15 Heroines (Jermyn Street); Shebeen (& Nottingham Playhouse), Bad Blood Blues, King Hedley II (Theatre Royal, Stratford); All's Well That Ends Well, Romeo and Juliet (Shakespeare's Globe); Othello, Shakespeare Trilogy: Julius Caesar, Henry IV, The Tempest (Donmar); The House That Will Not Stand (Tricycle); Hopelessly Devoted (Birmingham Rep); Inheritance**
(Live!); All the Little Things We Crushed (Almeida); Mules (Young Vic); Arabian Knights (West End/International tour); Hyacinth Blue (Clean Break); Macbeth (Southwark Playhouse); Venetian Heat (Finborough); Hungry Ghosts (Tabard); Vibes From Scribes (Double Edge); The Wax King (Man in the Moon).**

Television includes: **The Count Of Monte Cristo, Dreaming Whilst Black, Pinch of Portugal, Casualty, Unforgotten, Dreamland, Sense And Sensibility, Shakespeare and Hathaway, The Bay, Eastenders, Jericho, The Dumping Ground, London's Burning, Coronation Street, Doctors, My Family, Missing, Shameless, Free Agents, Monday Monday, Little Big Mouth, A Touch of Frost, Always & Everyone, The Bill, A Wing & a Prayer, Peak Practice, Jonathan Creek, Dangerfield, Thief Takers, The Knock, The Governor, One for the Road, Little Napoleons, Harry, West Indian Women at War, Epiphany.**

Film includes: **Shrike, The Last Dance, The Little Mermaid, Summerland, Blitz, Forget Me Not, The Hurting, Dead Meat.**

Awards include: **Michael Elliott Trust Awards: Original Performance of the Year Screen Nation (BFM): Best Actress.**

Sam Curtis Lindsay
(Associate Director)

As director, theatre includes: **BURGERZ (& Edinburgh Festival Fringe/Traverse/ Southbank Centre), Waiting for Godot (Hackney Showroom); Tomorrow Is Already Dead (Soho); Oliver Cromwell is Really Very Sorry (Project Arts Centre); Class (Edinburgh Fringe/Home Manchester/ Theater Center Canada); The Court Must Have a Queen (Hampton Court Palace); Heartbreak Hotel (The Jetty Greenwich).** Awards include: **Total Theatre Award (BURGERZ).**

Christella Litras
(Composer & Musical Director)

Theatre includes: **Wind Rush-Movement of the People Phoenix, Nine Night, The Glass Slippes, Word Temple (Tour); Power (Opera-Northern Ballet Tour); The Princess and The Pea, Yellow is the Colour of Sunshine (Tutti Frutti/Tour); As You Like It, Romeo and Juliet, Fairy Poppins, Searching for the Heart of Leeds, 50 Years Celebration of King and Queen Show, Dubwise Lik, Dinner 18-55, Ruffwell Scandals, Heartbeat Riddim Chant, Come Skank Wid I, Buglight, Living Stories, First Cut, Queen Of Chapeltown (Leeds Playhouse); Down In The Dumps, Misrepresented People (Nottingham Playhouse); The Legends of Them (Brixton House); The Awakening (Headingly Stadium); Aladdin (Cast, Doncaster); Dance Vignettes (Phoenix Dance Theatre); Taking a Position (Riley Theatre); Sorrel and Black Cake (RJC Dance Theatre); Battle Dream Chronicles Resonance Residency (Opera North); Speak Out The (Carriageworks); Turn It Up Stage play (The New Art Exchange); Topfoto (The North Wall Gallery); Cheiftancy (Seven Arts Theatre); Snow Black and Rose Red (Stratford East); Ye-Ye Choreographic Platform (Yorkshire Dance); Message In a Bottle (Sadler's Wells); Travel Light (South Asain Arts UK, Chapel FM Theatre).**

Film includes: **Tale of a Winter Solstice, Round My Way, The Power Five Documentary, Carnival Messiah, Windrush Movement of the People, Battle Dream Chronicles, Naked Poet.**

Radio includes: **Sweet Dreams, Mr Herbert Zayne is Writing a Postcard Home.**

Awards include: **Best Score Animated Series, Multiple Animation Film Awards (Battle Dream Chronicles); Star Award Best Production (Windrush Movement of the People); Offie Award for Best Performance Piece (The Legends of Them); Ribbon Award-Contribution to the Arts; Local Hero Award-Service to the Community; Legacy Awards.**

Nina Lyndon
(Dramaturg & Co-Creator)

As producer, for the Royal Court: **Royal Court Young Writers Festival 2002, 2004, 2007 & 2009.**

As dramaturg, theatre includes: **BURGERZ (& Edinburgh Festival Fringe/Traverse/ Southbank Centre), for all the women who thought they were mad (Hackney Showroom).**

Awards include: **Offie Award for Best Performance Piece (The Legends of Them), Total Theatre Award (BURGERZ).**

Jo McInnes
(Director & Co-Creator)

For the Royal Court: **Red Bud; Vera, Vera, Vera.**

Other theatre includes: **The Legends of Them (Brixton House); For All The Women Who Thought They Were Mad (Hackney Showroom); Valhalla (Theatre503); 36 Phone Calls (Hampstead); Can Hear You, This Is Not An Exit (RSC); Running on Empty (Probe/Soho); Christmas (Bush/Tape NVT, Brighton).**

Film includes: **Pornography 'Coming Up'.**

Awards include: **BBC Audio Drama Award for Best Original Single Drama (Sea longing), Offie Award for Best Performance Piece (The Legends of Them).**

Also works extensively as an actor.

Elena Peña
(Sound Designer)

For the Royal Court: **Blue Mist, Baghdaddy, Two Palestinians Go Dogging, Seven Methods of Killing Kylie Jenner, Maryland, Living Newspaper.**

Other theatre includes: **A Tupperware of Ashes, The Hot Wing King, Trouble In Mind, Sweat, Nora: A Doll's House, Macbeth, Mountains, Rockets And Blue Lights Brainstorm (& Company3), (National); The Wedding Band (Lyric Hammersmith); Liberation Squares, The Memory of Water (Nottingham Playhouse); Cinderella (Brixton House); The Magic Finger (Unicorn); As You Like It (RSC); Wuthering Heights (China Plate/UK Tour); Songs Across the Sueniverse (Sherman); Misty (Shed NYC); Silence (Donmar/Tara); The Chairs (Almeida); Seven Methods of Killing Kylie Jenner (Riksteatern, Sweden); The Darkest Part of The Night, Reasons (You Shouldn't Love Me); Snowflake, The Kilburn Passion, Arabian Nights (Kiln); The Remains of the Day (Royal and Derngate); Autoreverse (BAC); Misty (& West End),**

Going Through, HIR, Islands (Bush); Thick As Thieves (Clean Break).

Melissa Simon-Hartman
(Costume Designer)

Theatre includes: **Lajables (Martinique Theatre Tour); Much Ado About Nothing (RSC); Once on this Island (Regent Park); Legends of Them (Brixton House).**

THE ROYAL COURT THEATRE

The Royal Court Theatre is the writers' theatre. It is a leading force in world theatre for cultivating and supporting writers - undiscovered, emerging and established.

Since 1956, we have commissioned and produced hundreds of writers, from John Osborne to Mohamed-Zain Dada. Royal Court plays from every decade are now performed on stages and taught in classrooms and universities across the globe.

Through the writers, the Royal Court is at the forefront of creating restless, alert, provocative theatre about now. We open our doors to the unheard voices and free thinkers that, through their writing, change our way of seeing.

We strive to create an environment in which differing voices and opinions can co-exist. In current times, it is becoming increasingly difficult for writers to write what they want or need to write without fear, and we will do everything we can to rise above a narrowing of viewpoints.

Through all our work, we strive to inspire audiences and influence future writers with radical thinking and provocative discussion.

🐦 royalcourt 📘 royalcourttheatre

Supported using public funding by
**ARTS COUNCIL
ENGLAND**

HACKNEY SHOWROOM

"Hackney Showroom delivers spellbinding theatre alongside enriching community building, culminating in a unique excellence that is hard to match" Gay Times

Hackney Showroom is an award-winning theatre company and grassroots civic arts venue led by Sam Curtis Lindsay and Nina Lyndon. As a home for experimental and genre-defying theatre, we work with innovative artists, offer them a rigorous approach to developing their practice, and collaborate with them on producing new work that changes the landscape of tomorrows theatre.

We tour work nationally and internationally, working with a myriad of communities to which we offer a warm and refreshing invitation to encounter live cultural experiences. Our venue on Kings Crescent Estate creates the best conditions for artists and locals to flourish, with a cultural community programme that forms bonds across our locale and an artist development programme that paves the way for artists to make astonishing and memorable work.

Hackney Showroom productions include: Tomorrow Is Already Dead by Ms Sharon le Grand, for all the women who thought they were mad by Zawe Ashton, BURGERZ by Travis Alabanza (winner, Total Theatre Award) and Frau Welt by Peter Clements & Oliver Dawe.

@hackneyshowroom

BRIXTON HOUSE

Brixton House is a modern arts venue in South London. An inspired vision to build a cultural hub centred on the legacy of the former Ovalhouse Theatre. The new multi-arts venue, with a particular focus on theatre, tells stories from undervalued, unheard voices and excluded communities.

A place for people to come together to create and enjoy performance, the venue houses two theatres and performance spaces, seven rehearsal rooms, meeting rooms, of!ce space dedicated to creative organisations as well as a public cafe and bar. Brixton House is generously supported by London Borough of Lambeth, Arts Council England, Gar!eld Weston Foundation, The Wolfson Foundation, Cockayne Grants for the Arts, London Community Fund, The 29th May 1961 Charitable Trust.

ROYAL COURT SUPPORTERS

Our incredible community of supporters makes it possible for us to achieve our mission of nurturing and platforming writers at every stage of their careers. Our supporters are part of our essential fabric – they help to give us the freedom to take bigger and bolder risks in our work, develop and empower new voices, and create world-class theatre that challenges and disrupts the theatre ecology.

To all our supporters, thank you. You help us to write the future.

PUBLIC FUNDING

Supported using public funding by
ARTS COUNCIL ENGLAND

CHARITABLE PARTNERS

The Common Humanity Arts Trust

BackstageTrust

COCKAYNE

T. S. ELIOT FOUNDATION

JERWOOD FOUNDATION

CORPORATE SPONSORS & SUPPORTERS
Aqua Financial Ltd
Cadogan
Concord Theatricals
Edwardian Hotels, London
NJA Ltd. – Core Values & Creative Management
Prime Time
Sustainable Wine Solutions
Walpole

SIS TER

CORPORATE MEMBERS
Bloomberg Philanthopies
Sloane Stanley

TRUSTS & FOUNDATIONS

Maria Björnson Memorial Fund
Martin Bowley Charitable Trust
Bruce Wake Charitable Trust
Chalk Cliff Trust
The Noël Coward Foundation
Cowley Charitable Foundation
The Davidson Play GC Bursary
Garrick Charitable Trust
The Lynne Gagliano Writers' Award
The Harold Hyam Wingate Foundation
John Lyon's Charity
The Marlow Trust
Clare McIntyre's Bursary
Old Possum's Practical Trust
Richard Radcliffe Charitable Trust
Rose Foundation
The Royal Borough of Kensington & Chelsea Arts Grant
Royal Victoria Hall Foundation
Theatres Trust
The Thistle Trust
The Thompson Family Charitable Trust

INDIVIDUAL SUPPORTERS

Artistic Director's Circle

Katie Bradford
Jeremy & Becky Broome
Clyde Cooper
Debbie De Girolamo &
Ben Babcock
Dominique & Neal Gandhi
Lydia & Manfred Gorvy
David & Jean Grier
Charles Holloway OBE
Linda Keenan
Andrew Rodger and Ariana
Neumann
Jack Thorne & Rachel Mason
Sandra Treagus for
ATA Assoc. LTD
Eric Abraham
Anonymous

Writers' Circle

Chris & Alison Cabot
Cas Donald
Robyn Durie
Héloïse & Duncan Matthews KC
Emma O'Donoghue
Maureen & Tony Wheeler
Melanie J. Johnson
Nicola Kerr
Anonymous

Directors' Circle

Piers Butler
Fiona Clements
Professor John Collinge
Julian & Ana Garel-Jones
Carol Hall
Dr Timothy Hyde
Anonymous

Platinum Circle

Moira Andreae
Tyler Bollier
Katie Bullivant
Anthony Burton CBE
Matthew Dean
Emily Fletcher
Beverley Gee
Damien Hyland
Susanne Kapoor
David P Kaskel &
Christopher A Teano
Peter & Maria Kellner
Robert Ledger &
Sally Moulsdale
Frances Lynn
Mrs Janet Martin
Andrew McIver
Brian & Meredith Niles
Corinne Rooney
Anita Scott
Bhags Sharma
Dr Wendy Sigle
Brian Smith
Mrs Caroline Thomas
Sir Robert & Lady Wilson
Beverley Buckingham
The Edwin Fox Foundation
Lucy and Spencer De Grey
Madeleine Hodgkin
Barbara Minto
Timothy Prager
Sir Paul & Lady Ruddock
James and Victoria Tanner
Yannis Vasatis
Anonymous

With thanks to our Silver and Gold Supporters, and our Friends and Good Friends, whose support we greatly appreciate.

Let's be friends. With benefits.

Our Friends and Good Friends are part of the fabric of the Royal Court. They help us to create world-class theatre, and in return they receive early access to our shows and a range of exclusive benefits.

Join today and become a part of our community.

Become a Friend (from £40 a year)

Benefits include:
- Priority Booking
- Advanced access to £15 Monday tickets
- 10% Bar & Kitchen discount (including Court in the Square)

Become a Good Friend (from £95 a year)

In addition to the Friend benefits, our Good Friends also receive:
- Five complimentary playtexts for Royal Court productions
- An invitation for two to step behind the scenes of the Royal Court Theatre at a special event

Our Good Friends' membership also includes a voluntary donation. This extra support goes directly towards supporting our work and future, both on and off stage.

To become a Friend or a Good Friend, or to find out more about the different ways in which you can get involved, visit our website: royalcourttheatre. com/support-us

The English Stage Company at the Royal Court Theatre is a registered charity (No. 231242)

Lorna Gee: with Ricky Ranking winning the sound clash for Harris Sound, Nasty Rockers 1998; at the New York Tamika Reggae Awards 1992; with Buju Banton, 1992.

Stills from Sutara's home video archive, shown in the final scene: Sutara at the retreat in India having her hair cut by Mooji; climbing the Arunachala mountain to burn her locks; a conch being blown on the side of the mountain.

The Legends of Them

'There is one earth, but billions of worlds.'

Mooji

Sankofa

From the Twi language of Ghana, meaning 'go back and fetch it';
we must look back to the past so that we understand how we
became what we are and move forward to a better future.

Satsang

A satsang is a gathering and a Sanskrit word meaning 'the
company of truth'. A satsang can include meditation, discussion,
chanting and listening to spiritual teachings. People of different
levels of experience can practice together.

Author's Note

I want to thank all those who helped to make this possible, including Helen Comerford and Paul Bourne. Special thanks to Nina Lyndon and Jo McInnes, we became the three degrees of inseparation!

Thanks also to all the people that supported me and encouraged me on this journey.

Finally, I'd like to thank the legends in my life: my mother Euphemia who came from Jamaica in the 1950s with nothing, and gave us everything; my sister Cherry who was my hero; my brother Mooji who has guided me all my life on this earthly plain and the spiritual; and my son Nathan Fagan Gayle who gave my life more meaning.

When the mind comes, let it.

Sutara

Characters

Lorna

The Legends
Ma, *mother*
Cherry, *sister*
Nanny, *ancestor*
Tony/Mooji, *brother*

Globe
Police Officer
Nicola
Karen
Pastor
Lorna's siblings
Uncle Les
Sally
Taxi Driver
White Man
Prosecutor
Psychiatrist
Harris
Dominoes players
Red Eye
Linton Kwesi Johnson
Big Foot Carmen
Tony Williams
Holloway Girls
Big John
Mercedes
Q Club MC
Church Voices
Miss Stye
Spunky

Sutara

Notes

// Denotes overlap.

All characters are conjured in memory. For the Hackney Showroom production at Brixton House and the Royal Court Theatre, Sutara witnesses these memories live on stage as well as experiencing them through a riverbed of sound and film. All characters are voiced by Sutara with the exception of Mooji whose real voice we hear.

This text went to press before the end of rehearsals and so may differ slightly from the show as performed.

Darkness. Overture.

Voices coming out of the overture.

Sounds of India.

Lorna   You're not good enough for this, remember?

Lorna *appears in a spotlight. She is dripping in sweat.*

Slipping off the edge
Slipped into the empty void
Can't catch a grip
Nothing to hold on to
Stomach churning
Chest tight
Shallow breaths
Hard to breathe
Palpitations

Devastation

She looks down and sees a microphone in her hands.

A riverbed of resonance underscores throughout.

(*Song.*) This happens to be Lorna Gee the original British
born Brixtonian out of town from London harfdread
barlhead, artical funky deadlocks from London England //

Superstar!
Hanging wid de creme of the crop an mi have
Pretty car
Money ah flow, me a do nuff show
Near and far
No mess wid de halfdread barlhead or there will be war
Dis here Windrush baby yes mi come from far
Star, rah, hear me now

This a Lorna Gee with the mic in my han'
Anywhere me go me have fe rock deh session
Whether Brooklyn, Bronx or Brixton
People this is one thing you have to try to understand

My name is Lorna Gee and I am what I am
What people say I don't care I don't give a damn
Me no want praise me no want pity me not want contention
When me chatting pon the mic me chat the right and not the wrong
Jalaman Jalaman Jalaman say we are born champion
Jalaman Jalaman Jalaman say we are born champion //

Globe   Hey yo Larna

Lorna   Globe. Globe! Globe oh my God. Big man promoter. Big man in the business. Wha gwarn Globe.

Globe   Wha gwarn Larna. You waan mek some real money?

Lorna   Who you talking to me? I'm already making money. I'm opening for Shabba Ranks

Globe   You deserve it too. You no stay like de other girls, you ballsy. That's why me giving you a chance fe mek some real money.

Lorna   Oh. My. God! Are those real Rolexes? Are these all 100 dollar bills?

Globe   How you ask so much question? Furthermore, Globe don't wear nutten fake. All you need to know is there's more where that come from. But me no know if you ready fi dem kinda moves.

Lorna   I was born ready. This happens to be Lorna Gee the original British born //

Globe   I put you on the biggest stage shows and put money in your pocket and me never even see the colour of your drawers yet.

Lorna   This happens to be Lorna Gee //

Nicola   You didn't come home again last night. I know you're sleeping with him. Don't lie to me.

Lorna   I'm not sleeping with Globe, he's my promoter.

Nicola   Well, all y'all are spending plenty time together.

Lorna   Look Nicola, my dick days are well and truly over, so you ain't got nothing to worry about. Besides, ain't nutten hot like my Guyanese pepperpot!

Nicola   Then why you introduce me to your artist friends? You just keep me in the hotel like I'm some frikkin side chick.

Lorna   I'm in the reggae industry. They don't take kindly to the lesbian lifestyle. An you wanna come hold my hand and kiss me up in front of dem man deh! Nahh man!

(*Song.*) This happen to be Lorna Gee the original British born
Brixtonian out of town from London harfdread barlhead //

Globe   Wha gwarn Larna.

Lorna   Wha gwarn Globe.

Globe   See dat big package over dere? Me send you pon de coach to Texas and a man will meet you at de udder side ah de coach station.

You feel you can handle it?

Lorna   I can handle anything.

(*Song.*) This happen to be Lorna Gee the original British born
Brixtonian out of town //

Police Officer   Ma'am, ma'am hold it right there please

Lorna   What's going on officer

Police Officer   Just a regular security check ma'am. Can you tell me which one is your bag?

Lorna   Oh . . . erm . . . that one, there's my bag, it's filled with British gifts for my aunt in Texas. I'm from England you see, in case you didn't notice. She loves all the name brands. I got PG Tips tea bags, Cadbury's Fruit and Nut

chocolate, Kellogg's corn flakes, Heinz baked beans and
Marks and Spencer's knickers. She loves all that stuff. You
can have a look if you like.

Pause.

Police Officer   That's OK, ma'am. Move right along.

Lorna (*song*)   This happens to be Lorna Gee the original
British
born Brixtonian out of town from London harfdread //

Nicola   Why would you throw your whole career away for a
little extra cash.

Lorna   What career? Remember, Nicola. They're never
gonna let me be a Shabba or Buju. I'm just a token.

(*Sings.*) This happens to be Lorna Gee the original British
born Brixtonian out of town from London harfdread //

Globe   Wha gwarn Larna.

Lorna   Wha gwarn Globe.

Globe   You waan mek even bigger money? White powder
like soft snow. (*Does a line.*) Now tek off your panty.

Lorna (*does a line*)   Not on your nelly, mate.

I've had it with Globe. I'm going independent. I'll start off
with half a key.

Beat.

Lorna   This happens to be //

Jamaica Avenue. Queens. Projects. Gotta get through the
bulletproof door. Gotta get past the papita and his gun.
They don't know me from Adam. Am I gonna come out
alive?
Yo, I never cut it with anything, this is pure Colombian.

(*Song.*) This hallen to be Lorna Gee the original British Born
Brixtonian out of town from London harfdread //

You want this eight ball or not?

Excuse me, scuse me . . . sorry, excuse me they've just called my name.

Oh my God, I can't believe it . . . I wasn't expecting this at all, I was in the reception eating chicken wings.

Thank you, Clinton Lindsay for this New York Tamika Reggae Award for best female DJ. Thank you. Oh my God. Thank you.

Big up to all the other girls in the same category. Sister Carol, respect queen; Sister Charmaine, bless up; Shelley Thunder, some man fe get koof! And Lady Patra. You should've won. I can't believe it.

I used to listen to all of you chat on the mic on cassette tapes. And coming here to America I get a chance to perform on stage with my teachers.

Big up Man like Shabba Ranks, I see you!
Big dutty stinkin Shabba Rankin:
You should hear the likkle girl dem sing, wha dem sing

(*Song.*) Ting-a-ling a ling, school bell a ring
Knife and fork ah fight fi dumplin
Booyaka! Booyaka! Call for Shabba Rankin
Shabba Ranks jus' appear and tear annadda man chin through
Dem a di don, to di biz we ave di key
Put do don to di key and turn him inna donkey

And look there, one of my greatest teachers, the one and only Ninja Man:

(*Song.*) Me ah goh
Murder dem, murder dem
In a competition me ah go murder dem
Murder dem, murder dem
In a competition him ah go murder dem
The front teet, gold teet, gun pon teet Don Gorgon

Nice to see you sitting beside the 'Don Dadda' himself
Supercat:

(*Song.*) Don Dadda
Fi all DJ Mr Cat a Don Dadda
Run go tell yuh sista and yuh bredda and modda
No buoy can't test Mr Cat and falla
And wat a ting when I put down the mic and Mr Tenor Saw
pick it up
People are you ready?
Blow! Oh lawd
Are you ready for Tenor Saw medley?
Blow! Oh lawd

Tick a tick a toc my golden hen
She laying eggs for the gentlemen
Sometimes nine and sometimes ten, hey
And wherever she lay she raise an alarm
Ca ca ca ca ca layo
Lay ay ay ay ay ay oh oh
Lay oh oh ay //

Sound of the crack pipe.

(*Spoken.*) Cut it up
Spoon it up
Cook it up
Bagi it up
And . . .

Sound of the crack pipe.

Karen   Hey, Pedro said you sued to be a reggae star.

Lorna   Pedro needs to stop freebasing (*She laughs
maniacally.*)

(*Tries to sing.*) This happen to be Lorna Gee the original
British born Brixtonian out of town from London
harfdread barlhead article funky dreadlock from
London England

This happen to be Lorna Gee the original British born
Brixtonian out of town from London harfdread barlhead
article
funky dreadlock from London England

This happen to be Lorna Gee the original British born
Brixtonian out of town from London

This happens to be Lorna Gee

(*Spoken.*) This happens to be
This happens to be
This happens to be
This happens to be
Crack
Slipping off the edge
Slipped into the empty void
Can't catch a grip
Nothing to hold on to
Stomach churning
Chest tight
Shallow breaths
Hard to breathe
Palpitations

Devastation

*Silence. All resonance stops. We are in Lorna's room at the silent
retreat.*

Mooji   Beloved one.

Lorna   Mooji. My brother, my big brother.

Help.

Mooji   I have something to share with you. Right now.

Don't judge anything, let everything just be. Just like you
are, right here now.

Lorna   I don't understand.

Mooji   There is a stillness inside you that has been here since the beginning of time

You are aware of yourself. You know that you exist, naturally. All this world you can see. The sense of smell, of taste, of sight, of hearing, of feeling. Discover that space of pure emptiness.

Lorna *switches a lamp on.*

Lorna   The bed is on the left. And all around, there's windows, kind of like . . . small windows that open. There's a little stove on the sink on the right there. There's a rug and two straw chairs under the window. There's a fan. It's a ceiling fan. No. a standalone fan. And like, not a dresser, but a ledge. A stone ledge where you can put your belongings.

Why have I packed high heel shoes to come to India? And a ghetto blaster? Don't kid yourself, go back to New York and sing songs. You're famous.

I'm a has been.

Mooji   The power to remember, or to know things, all of this is with you. And you are not to reject anything at all. Don't judge anything, let everything just be. Just like you are, right here now. Let everything that happened happen.

Pause.

Lorna   You're not good enough for this, remember?

Silence.

Ma   You're my daughta and ah love you and ah will always love you.

Ma *humming a song.*

Lorna (*recalling the song*)   Oh hand me down, hand me down my silver trumpet Gabriel . . .

Pastor   Today at Sabbath school we shall lift up our voices in exaltation. Now I want someone to sing a song . . .

Lorna *puts up her hand.*

Pastor   Other than Miss Lorna

Lorna (*song*)   . . . hand me down my silver trumpet
L.O.R.D.

Ma   Sing de song like everybody else before me pinch orf
yu lip. Why you have to be so extra?

Lorna   Sorry, Ma

Pastor   Remember the sabbath day to keep it holy, six days
shalt thou labour, and do all thy work: 'But the seventh day
is the sabbath of the Lord thy God: in it thou shalt not do
any work.'

Ma   And that means none whatsoever. No shopping, no
cooking, no music. You can read. . . but only the Bible, or
better still, an Ellen G. White pamphlet.

Piece of chocolate for you Cherry, piece for you Pauline,
Piece for Mooji, piece for Martin, piece for Mervyn, piece for
Danny, piece for you Lorna, piece for Julie.

And this likkle piece of chocolate for Les.
I'll leave it in the fridge for him.

Lorna   Why did he deserve a piece, Ma?

Ma   Because he was my husband, Lorna

Lorna   But why didn't you fight back?

Ma   I worked and slave to buy that house on Haycroft road
with m own money in 1958 so you could all be safe.

The first notes of **Ma**'s *song.*

I groomed you all in God, made with love I bore eight
children, four boys, four girls
Mooji, Cherry and Pauline born in Jamaica and five of you
in England

(*Song.*)   So Brixton was to be my nurturing ground
It wasn't easy but I did my best
Had three jobs on the go without no rest
And restless you all became without your mammy
I had to pack it in and stay at home
Couldn't bear to leave you children anymore
So I continued with my trade
All the fancy dresses I made
My sewing machine was to become my ninth child!

Vroom vroom
The sound rang through every room
I sewed day and night for factory pickings

The orders came flooding in
For dresses, pants, slips and things
And my children always had the latest fashion

I found God in Brixton Seventh Day Adventist Church

And I found everything else in Brixton Market
It had the flavour of my homeland, Jamaica
Yam, dasheen, banana, coco, okra, cassava
Plus, Everything I needed to clean
Dettol, Ajax, Windolene

Everybody stops to talk to me
For i'm a pillar of the community
If I don't mind sharp
I'll be here in Brixton all day

Last stop, material shop,
Two thimbles, pack of needles
Fifteen zip, let me stock
All for my precious sewing machine
All for my precious sewing . . .

(*Screaming.*) Murder! Murder! Murder!

Lorna   Uncle Les is home
Uncle Les is home
His knee on her chest

Strangling her
Gonna kill her this time

Siblings   Close your eyes
Block your ears

Ma   Murder! Him going to kill me

Lorna   Switch the light on
Bad things happen in the dark
Here comes the bogeyman

Siblings   Uncle Les is drunk, push him off, Ma.

He will float off you like a piece of paper

Uncle Les   Lorna, sit down and shut up.

Hush up your crying, all of you.

Lorna   Bad things always happen in the dark, d'you know what I mean? The Bogey Man and all of these kinds of things, it's always going to just come in the dark . . .

Mooji   Suppose you could not retain anything in memory? Suppose you could not retain anything in memory? Everything has to be used up now. Nothing to keep in the fridge. Would anything trouble you? Because for most people, their life is memory. Our deep attachment is to memory.

Lorna   I can't not remember.

(*Song.*)   School number one
Stockwell Manor
Noh good grammar
Fish outta wata
A likkle terror
Dem caal har Larna
Dem try to tame har
Name and shame har
As a teenager
She was a hustler

De time waster
Da game player

(*Spoken.*) Heads or tails? Heads or tails?
What? You trying to say I'm cheating?

(*Song.*)   Hol har back
She might attack
De temper what she have
No have no match
Stan ah back
Teacher chat
Wait a minute
Who are you?

Sally   Alright Laura, d'you wanna make some real money?

Lorna   My name's Lorna not Laura

Sally   Lorna, Laura, hunky Dora! Who cares?

Lorna   Wait. So what do you call real money?

Lorna (*song*)   And then my Mada get a phone call
From Babylon say me get charge
Because we teef Mr Raj car
And Sally run lef me on guard

Oh lawd have mercy mercy mercy
Now mummy ah go beat me beat me beat
An no school in a de country country country
Ago grant me any entry entry entry

School number two,
Dick Sheppard
Dirty Dicks
Full of tricks
Pure gal inna de mix
Wrong ends
You getting drape-up
Gimme yu ring

Noh seh nuttin
Gimme yu ring
I not playing
Snatch yu chain
Nah no shame
Keep calm
Wrong uniform

Fool fool gal
Inna my neighbourhood
We ago beat you down
We a beat you, beat you down good

Den headteacher get de newsflash
Seh we sell de ring fe likkle cash
An den me mada get de phone call
Seh yu daughter is a downfall

Oh lawd have mercy mercy mercy
Dis pickney ah go kill me kill me kill me
No school inna de country country country
Ago grant yu any entry entry entry

School number three
School for the Maladjusted
Miss, what does maladjusted mean?

School number four
St Joseph's Boarding School,
Chippenham Mews, Marshfield, Bath, Wiltshire

Sounds of car and sheep.

Lorna   Where we going? Timbuktu?

Taxi Driver   Where have you's come from then?

Ma (*in her best posh accent*)   Lindin!

Taxi Driver   Where?

Ma   Er . . . Lindin

Lorna   She means London. Mum, just talk normal (Ow!) Hey Steve, where's all the black people man? This place looks like the Twilight zone. I ain't staying ere.

(*Song.*)   St Joseph's
Cath-o-lic
Pure Nuns
Inna Habit
Favour Penguin
Biscuit
No no
Me nah go fit
Motorway
Me a go hitch

Sounds of car screeching and a man yells.

White Man   Nigger nigger pull the trigger, bang bang bang!

Prosecutor   I would reluctantly suggest, therefore, that the court consider granting a care order to London Borough of Lambeth with suggested recommendations for a contained environment where outside influence can be strictly controlled for this girl.

Pause.

Psychiatrist   Lorna, isn't it? My name's Dr Gately, I'm the Resident Psychiatrist here at Middlesex Lodge. I'm here to help you. I'm on your side.

Lorna   Is it?

Psychiatrist   Now Lorna, I'm going to ask you a series of questions, please answer concisely and clearly. If your mother sent you to buy a loaf of white bread but the shop didn't have any, what would you buy instead?

Pause.

OK. Let's try another one. What's the difference between an orange and a lemon?

Pause.

Lorna   Ma. I'm sorry. Please. Let me come home.

Ma   It's not me who put you there, you know Lorna. It's the court's decision. There's nothing more I can do. Only God can save you now.

Lorna   I've had enough of this, home.

Bass vibrations start.

> **Mooji**   Whose is this vulnerability? You will come to see that the vulnerable one is this imagined self, the imaginary self.

Huge bass vibration.

Lorna   The Blue Lagoon, Railton Road, Brixton. It's pitch black, thick ganja smoke in the air. All I can see is the whites of people's eyes. One way in and one way out. Sharon brought me here. We're thirteen but no one's checking. The bassline captures your soul at any age. It penetrates your heart. The vooooom lifted me off the ground! There is no lie here. This is true, honest Reggaefication! Here, we are one. It's just me and the bass. This is my sanctuary. This is my escape.

Ma   What time ah marnin you caal dis? You mean to seh you climb outta de window like a teif in de miggle of de night, fe go ah devil dance? You tink me wouldn't fine out? You tink me born dis big?

Lorna   Sorry Ma, I won't do it again!

Ma (*calling after her*)   What happened to you Larna? You use to be such a good Christian girl. You could've become a missionary, the way you know you Bible. What happened to you?

Cherry   You can't know yourself unless you know where you come from.

Lorna   22 Normandy Road. I knew every crack in the pavement to my sister Cherry's house. From Stockwell Park Estate, go down Robsart Street, take a left onto Brixton Road, second on the right.

The bass bleeds into the sound of dominoes. **Cherry**'s *kitchen full of the sounds of Bob and Marcia.*

Domino Players   Six love! Double deuce!

Cherry   You all are welcome to my house. Eat food, and drink and play dominoes. Sense of belonging is what we've got. But mek sure when you come here you no chat no fraff.

Domino Players   Blank ah blank yu ave! Weh yu have? Ah blank yu have? Eh? Eh? Ah blank yu ave? Watch ya now! Oonu don't have no status, oonu don't deserve to be in a Cherry house! Oonu ready? Oonu no ready! Hol on deh, seet ya now . . . Bam! (*Bang of last domino.*) Six love!

Cherry   Red Eye, why you affi mek up so much rarse noise?

Everytime you come here you do the same ting!

Red Eye   Sorry Miss Cherry

Cherry   Red Eye, you tek your medication this morning? Me ah put your food in a Tupperware Red Eye, com go ah you yard and next time you come here, mek sure yu tek you medication first because you too loud!

Red Eye   Me born loud, it's the way me tark, noh mean say me mad

Lorna   Cherry, where do I come from?

Cherry   You come from our mada

Lorna   No, where do I really come from? What is my roots? You know all the Jamaican stories.

Cherry   I can tell you everything about Port Antonio where me barn. And Comfort Castle where ya mada barn. I can tell you about the Blue Lagoon, the Maroons, the Blue Mountains, which part you wana know?

Lorna   The Blue Mountains.

Cherry   Alright.
Six love! You lose, me win!

Red Eye   Woi oyoi.

Cherry   Mum mever tell you bout Nanny of the Maroons?

Lorna   No

Cherry   Is de Obeah she fraid of. That generation noh like talk bout dem history. Dem forget it's the magic that help liberate we from slavery. Dem only want to big up de queen of England.

Lorna   What's Obeah?

Cherry   Obeah is a inner knowledge, a natural power what Nanny possessed.

Nanny *casts her shadow over the room.*

Nanny   Listen to me and listen to me good. I, Queen Nanny of the Maroons was born in the Motherland Africa, from the Ashanti tribe. And when the British stole us from the Gold Coast and put us pon a slave ship to Jamaica, I escaped, freed over a thousand enslaved people and we run up into the hills of the blue mountains of Portland. That's how I and my warriors overthrew the British and tek up settlement where they call Mooretown.

Cherry   She knew how to ward off evil and protect her warriors from the British. She could cast spells using plants and herbs.

Lorna   They never teach me any of this at school.

Cherry   That's because they don't want you to know 'bout your history. Moore Town is where our mother was born. We are of the Maroon people. You can't know yourself unless you know where you've come from. You have the strength of a lion.

Lorna   No I haven't.

Nanny   My troops are masters of camouflage. We are trees that come to life and pounce on the British soldiers! The breath of my warriors is so slowed that the enemy never hears us coming. I can catch a bullet with one hand and return it back to my attacker!

Strength runs through your veins.

Ma   I don't want to hear none of that devil music

Lorna   But Mum!

Ma   Dem boof baf music not going to play inna this house, not on my gram

Lorna   But Mum, how can you put Jim Reeves over Burning Spear?

Ma   Lorna, I want you to stop this foolishness and get yourself a job.

Lorna   Ma, I want to be a singer.

Ma   A proper job. If you want to sing, sing for de Lord.

Linton   Lorna G!

Lorna   Linton Kwesi Johnson! Beg yu a cigarette

Linton   How you wuk and you sweat, til you have short breath and you still a beg people cigarette?

Lorna   I'm broke man! I've just come from the dole office, I've been waiting three whole weeks for my Giro and it still ain't come.

Linton   What about the music?

Lorna   I've been asked to make this record with the Mad Professor but I ain't got enough lyrics for a whole song.

Linton   You see what you just tell me bout your Giro . . . write about that.

Ma (*shouting over music*)   You're a bright girl. You can be a lawyer, a doctor or an engineer, if you just put your mind to it. Why don't you start off with the Youth Opportunities Scheme. They can teach you a real trade and they pay you £26.50 a week.

Lorna (*song*)   I worked at Pizza Hut, Pizza Land,
Pizza Palace, Pizza van,
Wimpy, Micky Dees, Burger King, Kentucky
Tired of di food chain
Getting fat, change de game
Office work, no work fe me
Boss ah tek pure liberty
Look pon big woman like me
Ah tell me muss go mek tea
Ain't no shame in my game
Let mi try da hotel chain
Chambermaid, bed maid,
Fold the sheets, underneath
Supervisor love scream
YOU'RE NOT FOLDING EM PROPERLY
Run red, keep your bread
I scarcely make my own bed
This life is not for me
Ain't no creativity
Tesco, Sainsbury's, C&A, Kwik Save
Bingo, Lotto, security, not for me
Ma I've tried, Ma I've tried, never lied
Oh I've tried, yes I've tried
Oh I've tried, yes I've tried
Oh I've tried, yes I've tried

(*Spoken.*) Swallow your pride
Swallow your pride
Swallow your pride
Swallow your pride
Swallow your pride

There's certain rules
I can't abide
Not even Jesus Christ had a nine-to-five
So why should I, Ma, why should I?
Swallow your pride
Swallow your pride
Swallow your pride

Swallow your pride
Swallow your pride

> **Mooji**   You Everyone is troubled by something. Why are
> we troubled by things? Because you want them to be a
> certain way and they won't obey your desire.

Lorna   You're not good enough for this, remember?

Nothing go gain
Pain turns to shame
Stomach wrenching
Humliation

Shop alarm sounds loud.

Lorna   I was gonna pay for it. Let me go, you cunt!

Carmen   Welcome to Holloway, my girl.

Lorna   They're callin my name

Pain turned to shame

Stomach wrenching

Humiliation

Carmen   You got any tobacco?

Lorna   Jumpy Janet, What you doing here? Split Lip Susie,
Big Foot Carmen. Big Foot Carmen! Rar, ain't seen you lot
from time? Nah guy, you lot just went missing, so this is
where you been //

Tony Williams   Now you're about to hear a brand new
musical disc on Rockers FM. It's on Mad Professor's Ariwa
label, a track called Three Weeks Gone (Mi Giro), by a new
artist called Lorna Gee. Take a listen //

We hear **Lorna Gee** *'Three Weeks Gone (Mi Giro)'.*

Lorna (*over the song*)   Three weeks gone and mi Giro no
come
The other day me go to social to collect me lump sum

The man behind the bar told me just to hold on
This is one thing I'm telling each and everyone
Me never wait two minutes or two second
Me wait from ten til quarter to one
A little after that lord they sent a next man
The man sit down he started to frown
He said sorry love your Giro's not around //

*The **Girls** are banging on their cell doors.*

Girls   Lorna, you're on the radio!!! Woiiii, you're gonna be famous! Can I have your autograph //

A different vibration. We are back in the room.

Lorna   Unlovable

Unsafe

An imposter

A disgrace

> **Mooji**   You have nothing in the world to conquer more than your mind. You have nothing in the world to conquer or to challenge or to transcend apart from your mind. All your neighbours live here. Your enemies and friends live here. Your gods and demons live here. And your self imagined lives here.

A storm cracks through the window.

Big John   Lorna. Open up.

Silence.

Lorna. Open up. You want a piece of the snake?

> **Mooji**   Just keep witnessing the traffic of your mind. The witness has to stand apart. Just be aware. Don't be selective, just be.

Lorna   But I am where the memories come from. These things happened to ME. I can't just forget.

(*Echoing* **Mooji**.) I'm not asking you to forget. But to hold your memories with distance.

I can't forget what happened.

Big John   Lorna. Open up. Open up. You want a piece of the snake?

Lorna   Aright, Big John. Erm . . . What's a snake?

What was you doing in the boy's house in the first place?

Melting Pot Children's Home for the maladjusted, London Borough of Lambeth. I walk up the stairs. I see my bedren Bumper. It was like he knows something's was going to happen but he can't warn me because he's scared. I open the door. Bed on the left. Clothes piled up on armchair. The room is dimly lit. This doesn't feel right.

Big John   Gimme you hand. Feel it!

Lorna   Just let me go, I won't tell anyone, I promise.

Big John   If you tell anyone, no one is going to believe you. You're nothing but an old bed.

Lorna   Please let me go. I'm only thirteen.

Big John   If you don't shut up, I'll get my gun from under the bed.

Lorna   Transfixed. Eyes on the ceiling. heartbeat pumping in stereo. Is my time up? Will I die by the gun or the pain of this penetration?

Storm rumbles.

Lorna (*spoken, rising to song*)   Nar go let no man, tek no liberty wid me
This a man's world. Yeah?
Wait and see
Tink woman only good fi tek off dem panty
Bun ah fire pon de dutty bwoy weh mess wid me

Me ah go lock him in a box, carry you down a cemetery
And likkle after dat maggot dem nyam your buddy
You mess wid de wrong gal, you tek from de wrong gal
It's time for your burial, nah cry at your funral
If you want Larna G to go a likkle further
I beg you hole up you han and just barl MURDER!

Mooji   You have so much power. All the power is with you but we hand it to the mind, which tyranise your spirit, keeps you feeling divided because this is how it rules.

Pastor   Put your hands on her head and let us pray that the Lord forgives you for the sin of homosexuality.

Lorna   Don't touch my head.

Pastor   Let us pray for this sodomite girl.

Lorna   Let me go.

Pastor   Jezebel refused to repent of her immorality. And her fate was sealed.

Church Voices   Jesus loves you, he will forgive you.

Pastor   Sodom and Gomorrah indulged in sexual immorality and underwent the punishment of eternal fire.

Church Voices   Give yourself up to Jesus.

Lorna (*song*)   They call it a crush but I know that it's love
This is everything that I've been dreaming of
You're the first, the one and the only
And now I'll never ever be lonely
You're the first one to listen to me
my school teacher, you understand me
Oh, Miss Stye
Yeah, Miss Stye
The love I have for you will never die
You're the apple in my apple pie
The wind in my whistle, the Stye in my eye
Oh Miss Stye

Yeah, Miss Stye
The love I have for you will never die

Miss Stye   Why do you keep running away, my love? We
can go to Bristol then we can go watch Saturday Night Fever
and then I'll take you to meet my parents. Now, they don't
see many coloureds so if my dad calls you a coon, take no
notice, it's just his way . . . he doesn't mean anything by it.

Lorna   OK. Can I suck your tits, miss?

Pastor   Leviticus Chapter 18, Verse 22. You shall not lie
with a man as with a woman; it is an abomination.

MC   Yes crowd ah people, oonu ready? Me can't hear you,
me seh are you ready? (*Crowd responds.*) Well, right now, this
happens to be a special act coming up on stage. This is
SOMETING FOR THE MANDEM! So I want de man dem
to say 'Oi yoi!' (Oi yoi) and I want de woman to shout 'yeah
yeah' (yeah yeah) crowd ah people, light up you lighter,
stamp you feet, lick wood, for the most spectacular act to
come to the Q Club. All the way from the US of A . . . The
one and only . . .

Lorna   Long legs, big brown eyes, the smoothest golden
brown skin I've ever seen
Lips
Hips
Holy shit
She strips
She's a stripper!
And she's beautiful
First the top comes off
Then the bra, then off with the panties
She had me then
But then she does the fucking splits
Oh shit
Pinch me someone
Who am I?
Why am I?

Gawping at this
Ungodliness
Why is my heart
Beating like the Nyghbingi drums
I feel sick. I feel light. I feel ashamed. I feel. . .

(*To* **Mercedes**.) You were brilliant

Silence.

Mercedes   Why thank you, girls are not normally so complimentary. They always feel threatened that I'll take their man

Lorna   Oh, no worries there, I ain't got a one

Mercedes   Is that so? I'm surprised nobody ain't snapped you up, you kinda cute

Lorna   Y. . .you think so?

Mercedes   I'm gonna be at the Hideaway Club in Dalston, if you ain't too busy, why don't you come down. Just ask for Mercedes.

Lorna   Oh my God, I'm going to burn in hell.

The storm builds.

Church Voices   We're telling the devil get thee hence Satan! In the name of Jesus, GET THEE HENCE //

Lorna   Please God
Let me feel normal
Send me a guy
So I can live a lie
And Ma will be happy
Delroy
Junior
Dennis
Everton
Sugar
John

Soloman
Was the wisest man
But he couldn't hold on to this woman

Sick love
Nauseous love
Dark love
Dependant love
Hold me tender love
Don't throw me away love

Think of my heart love
What about every love song
Were they wrong?
Dark
Sordid
Greedy love
Empty soul
Spirit grabbers
Taken
Deceased

Lorna   Please God forgive me for what I'm about to do, I don't know any other way out.

Hospital bed. Naked. Tubes down my throat.

> **Mooji**   What does witnessing mean? It means the witness is never involved in the scene that it's witnessing. Because the moment you become involved in the scene, you become part of the scene. The witness has to stand apart. Just be aware in a kind of panoramic openness. Just be aware that you are seeing, but don't link in. Stay like this.

Rain.

Lorna   Cherry's house. I plait her hair and she talks and the children and I laugh. I'm making sure I scrape up every hair into the canerow.

Cherry   All that love that you give that girl, you have to give it to yourself. Nobody going to love you the way you could love yourself.

Just mek sure you noh mess up me hair yu noh.

Lorna   Cherry, you know I can plait man!

Follicle by follicle I plait. And just for that moment, all the pressures drift away.

Nanny *appears.*

Nanny   Lorna. When the Maroons were at the brink of starvation, I almost gave up and surrendered to the British. But I listened to the voice of my ancestors.

I will teach you how to regain your strength. Take this remedy of seresee, seamoss and sorrel. It will heal you and make you strong again. Yes ai.

Lorna   Bad things always happen in the dark, d'you know what I mean? The Bogey Man and all of these kinds of things, it's always going to just come in the dark . . . I mean, how ridiculous is that? I'm thinking to myself that I'm not occupying the same space when it's daytime, d'you know what I mean, this is just a different time! But, it's the same space, it's just, like . . . a different colour. I can do this. I can sleep with the light off.

She turns the light off.

Spunky   Hey Empress! Norris Anthony Fagan. Pleased to meet you!

Lorna   I know you, they call you Spunky

Spunky   What you need is a real man to treat you like a queen

Lorna   Is it? So who might that man be then?

A moment.

No wonder they call you Spunky!

Ma   Look Larna, is a boy

Lorna   I don't want to look

Ma   Take your child Lorna. Look at your beautiful baby.

Lorna   Ma, I don't deserve to be a mum.

Ma   Come, take your child. He's a gift from God and he came from your womb.

Let me tell you something Larna

(*Song.*)   When I was just a child
My own sweet mother died
Barely eight years old with no one at my side
Sent from pillar to post
Coast to coast
No fixed abode
Abandoned and neglected
Mistreated and rejected
Then I heard another voice
Giving me a brand new choice
She said come to England, here your mother's waiting

All onboard, all onboard,
Mother's calling us ashore
Call the women, call the men, call the children
We're coming home at last
Coming to the motherland
Where she's waiting to welcome us with open arms

Well as I stood to wave goodbye
And sing the children's lullaby
Told them I'll be back as soon as I could manage
I grab my grip and board the ship,
Not certain where I was to kip
But all I knew mother would be there with open arms

All onboard, all onboard, Mother's calling us ashore
Call the women, call the men, call the children
We're coming home at last

Coming to the motherland
Where She's waiting to welcome us with open arms

What is dis, my God?
Me can't see through de fog
The coat me buy ah Cayman island noh warm enough
Jeezus, my God,
Why hast thou forsaken us
Dem seh No Irish, No Blacks, No Dogs
Dem lie to us

Mumma, weh yu deh?
Mumma, yu tell me com, so me com
Mumma yu never tell me seh me ah go sleep ah ground
You said the streets were paved with gold
Me want go back home but how
Mi only come with just enough to see me through the winter

All onboard, all onboard, Mother's calling us ashore
Call the women, call the men, call the children
We're coming home at last
Coming to the motherland
Where she's waiting to welcome us with open arms
Where she's waiting to welcome us with open arms

(*Spoken.*) Here, take your son, my grandson
The next generation to come

Lorna *takes the baby.*

Lorna   Nathaniel Abraham Lauren Fagan Gayle.
Nathaniel – means a gift from God.
Thank you, Norris, for our beautiful son.

> **Mooji**   At some point you'll feel that the claustrophobia
> of all this worldly internal and external noise and it will
> soon start to drift away, as though the hands cannot
> quite touch you. Like they are receding. And somehow
> replaced by a kind of presence. You realise you've been
> numb and your feeling this for yourself is coming back.

Ma   Hello? Hello? Hello?

Lorna   Ma?

Ma   I was just thinking about you before you call.

Lorna   Ma, you always say the same thing.

Listen, Mum. I called you because I have something to tell you.

Ma   Oh God. Mek me sit down.

Lorna   Well, um, I just want to tell you that, ahm, I'm a lesbian. Ma, you still there?

Pause.

Ma   Well . . . What about the Bible?

Lorna   What about the Bible?

Ma   Well, you're my daughtah and ah love you and ah will always love you.

> **Mooji**   You feel a calm space. And that is the presence of God, in you. No one has to tell you that this is a higher feeling. Not your guru. Not your minister. Not your gurubaai. No one, no.

Lorna   Mooji, my big brother Tony. My first love. The last sibling to join us from Jamaica. When we went to pick him up at the airport, he didn't come out, they said his visa weren't right. When he came to live with us, Uncle Les knew he had no match. Everything became calm.

OK. I surrender. I'm going all the way. I'm gonna sit on the floor, like everybody else.

Video: BBC News footage Brixton uprising 1985.[1]

BBC Reporter   *(A/V)*   Fires are still burning in Brixton in South London after an evening of rioting. It began as a demonstration of anger after police had shot and seriously injured a woman while searching her house. Then a crowd

---

[1] BBC News footage of Brixton Uprising, 1985

attacked a police station and gangs of youths began burning and looting buildings. Thirty-one policemen and five civilians have been hurt.

BBC Reporter (*A/V*)   *At the corner of Coldharbour Lane a four storey building collapsed after being set alight by petrol bombs. The top three storeys were flats above a furniture shop but they were thought to be unoccupied.*

Video: ITN News footage 1985.[2]

ITN Reporter (*A/V*)   At 7am seven police armed with Smith and Wesson .38 revolvers raided this house in Brixton. Two entered with a search warrant looking for Michael Groce who wasn't there. Inside was only his mother and five children.

Ma (*A/V*)   Seven police came with two dog and burst the door. And she'd thought it was her daughter upstairs not feeling well and when she rush out to see what happened, the police . . . she, running back towards her bedroom and the police shoot her in her back, in her bedroom . . . twice.

Tony/Mooji (*A/V*)   The bullet has travelled downward passing through her lung and coming out at the back so it seemed like two wounds. It's also lodged in her spine, fragments of metal, also from the bullet.

Cherry   I don't want the attention. Me is a private woman. I don't want no picture tek and don't want me face in no paper.

What dem fighting for is not de same ting me fighting for. Me just want mek sure seh my children's not hungry and dem not cold and if I'm not around then I can't guarantee that . . . Tell the people dem don't riot in my name. I hate violence.

Nanny *appears.* **Nanny** *chants and ritually washes* **Cherry***.*

---

[2] ITN News footage, shooting of Cherry Groce, 1985

Nanny   Cherry, I'm sorry I wasn't able to catch the bullet. I tried to find you but they separated us good and well. I am here now, I will not leave you again. Focus on my song whilst I bathe you.

(*Sings.*)   La leh Mull-lo oo
La leh mulleh
Ni-eh-deh ka meh
Chah podomeh

La le ma-leh-maa
La leh Mull-lo oo
La leh mulleh
Ni-eh-deh ka meh
Chah podomeh
La le ma-leh-maa

They told you you will have a life expectancy of five years but you will live for much longer.

Cherry   Dem take out every bone out of me legs. Never give me any anaesthetic because I couldn't feel anything. So for two-and-a-half hours I watch the doctor saw my bones, just like a butcher saw meat.

Nanny *and* **Lorna**   Cherry, You will know your children's children and watch them grow. They will know your name. Everyone will know your name.

Nanny *leads the march to the police station.*

Video: March against police racism.[3]

Nanny   Listen to me and listen to me good. We are fighting a mighty war and we are winnin! Attack the plantations! We will become part of the trees and create fires that can't be seen. Our hair is plaited with coded messages. Tell no one of the codes. The trees have ears. . . We must stick together. We cannot become fragmented. There is strength in numbers. Listen to the sound of the abeng and you will find your way.

---

[3] Footage of a protest against racism in the Met Police, 1980s

Every individual deserves to walk this Earth, breathing the
same air, for free. We will claim back our air. We will
breathe.

We will claim back our air. We will breathe.

Lorna   I'm coming for freedom
I wanna be free
Whatever this is holding me
I'm going to be free from it.
What's the worst that's gonna happen?
Am I going to die?
Well?
Come on then, do your thing.
Do. Your. Thing . . .

Lorna *releases a primal scream.*

Lorna   Ahhhahhhahhh. Ahhhhhhhhhhhhhhhhhhhhhhhh.
Ah ah ah . . . ahhhhhhhhhhhhh!

Video: The words 'Close Your Eyes'.

> **Mooji**
> OK
> OK
> OK
> Empty, empty, empty
>
> Not holding anything
>
> Now we are going to look at just what remains now.
>
> No past. No future. No present now.
>
> Don't engage with anything at all for a moment.
>
> You're not a container of thoughts, feelings and emotions.
> You're not holding anything at all.
>
> Your history, everything, OK? There will remain that
> which cannot be moved, cannot be taken out.

Just be aware of 'here'. Without giving a shape to it. You are just 'here'. Conscious.

Now I want to ask some simple, simple question to you, from this place of here-ness.

May I ask you, whatever remains now, does it have any shape at all? Just now?

Is, whatever it is that is here, I'm just going to call it the 'is' or the 'is-ness', whatever just 'is'. Is it an object?

Is it a mood? Not a mood.

Is it a belief? Whatever is here. Is it a belief? No.

Is there any desire in it? Just this. Just this. Any desire? No.

This. Is there, spatially any limitations, some boundary beyond which it does not exist any more?

This that is here. Are you creating it, or it simply is?

Did it come? Does it have a name?

May I ask you, can 'this', can it be sick? Or depressed?

Can anyone own it? No. Was it born or created? Now I'm going to ask something. Can it die or be destroyed?

All that we perceive comes and goes.. Like clouds drifting in the unchanging sky.

What we have just, done together is to recognise the infinite sky-like awareness of yourself.

Video: Personal archive footage of **Mooji** *cutting* **Lorna**'s *locks.*

Video: Personal archive footage of **Sutara** *burning her locks.*

Lorna (*V/O*)   This is my dreadlocks burning. I'm on the Arunachala Mountain, the most sacred mountain in the world. One of them at least. And I've cut my hair, my dreads. And I figured I wanted to leave them here. And this is where I got the inspiration to cut them and just to forget about that identity, lose that identity. I've been identifying with my dreadlocks for so many many many years and everybody's been identifying me with them. Now I'm just me. They're gone. And I leave them here as a gift. And now I'm a crazy balhead! And I feel so free. So liberated. So light. Thank you God.

Sutara (*song*)   Got to find a way . . .

Got to find a way
Got to find a way
Got to find a way

Got to find a way to get where I've got to go
Got to find a way to show what I've got to show-oh
Got to find a way

The blueprint of my life
Queen Nanny of the Maroons
My mother Euphemia
My sister Cherry
and our brother Mooji
The Legends of Them

The journey won't stop until I take my last breath.

When the mind comes, let it.

Sound of a conch blowing.

For a complete listing of
Methuen Drama titles, visit:
www.bloomsbury.com/drama

Follow us on Twitter and keep up to date
with our news and publications
@MethuenDrama